DESIGN IN MUS.

DESIGN IN MUSIC

by

GERALD ABRAHAM

LONDON

OXFORD UNIVERSITY PRESS

NEW YORK   TORONTO

Oxford University Press, Ely House, London W. 1

GLASGOW NEW YORK TORONTO MELBOURNE WELLINGTON
CAPE TOWN IBADAN NAIROBI DAR ES SALAAM LUSAKA ADDIS ABABA
DELHI BOMBAY CALCUTTA MADRAS KARACHI LAHORE DACCA
KUALA LUMPUR SINGAPORE HONG KONG TOKYO

ISBN 0 19 317301 8

First published 1949
Fifth impression 1973

*Printed in Great Britain by
Butler & Tanner Ltd, Frome and London*

CONTENTS

ACKNOWLEDGEMENT

This attempt to explain to laymen, in simple terms and colloquial language, the principles of musical design originally appeared as a series of articles in *Hallé*, the organ of the Hallé Concerts Society, and I am indebted to its Editor for permission to reprint.

G. A.

I

THE NATURE OF THE PROBLEM

THE problem of design in music arises in a quite peculiar form ... The remark is trite. But it is so fundamental to any discussion of musical 'design', 'form', 'architecture', 'structure', or whatever we like to call it, that unless we remind ourselves of it constantly we are very likely to go wrong through seeing apparent parallels with the problems of design in the other arts. Actually the only other art with which there is anything like a real parallel is poetry, and as we shall soon see the major problems of musical design are after all very different from the problem of design in poetry. One other point must be made at the very beginning. I have deliberately used several words such as 'design' and 'structure' as if they are synonymous; they are commonly so used. But they are not really synonymous. Design in music arises *out* of the problem of constructing it.

If someone uses the word 'design' in conversation, not apropos of music or anything in particular, we tend to think of *visual* design, visual pattern. We do it so naturally that it is almost impossible to avoid carrying over some of the implications of visual pattern into other uses of the word 'design'. We all do it sometimes, however unconsciously, in thinking and talking about music, but in doing so we impinge on grievous error. 'Design' in the visual sense implies filling a space or covering a surface, often a defined or even a given space or surface. And that is true not only in the merely decorative arts, where the surface may be a table-leg or a vase; the imaginative painter, even so far as I know the most advanced modernist among painters, accepts the convention of a rectangular space to be filled. (He must accept *some* spatial convention.) When the surface is covered, the resultant design is all there at the same time; the eye takes it in as a whole, even if it goes on to pick out details for special study and enjoyment later. And the design itself will in nine hundred and ninety-nine cases out of a thousand be based, however remotely, on natural objects: the human body, landscape, leaves or flowers or parts of them. The architect, *mutatis mutandis*, does spatially what the painter does superficially. His basic convention, more freely modified than the painter's rectangle, is the box—which of course arose originally from the need of walls and roof to exclude wild beasts and wild weather. The arts of painter and architect, their problems of design, arise from the desire to cover their spaces or elaborate their boxes so as to satisfy the human eye.

Consider how different the musician's problem is. He has no definite space to fill; he has only indefinite time. We may also say that for all practical purposes he has no materials for design in nature or natural needs: nothing more tangible and definable than bird song. And his design, when he produces it, can be apprehended only moment by moment—with the help of memory to recall the moments that have gone by. Is that really design at all? We may be quite sure of one thing: the conception of design in music, the thought that a piece of music could be apprehended as a whole, as a shape, is a relatively late conception in the history of music. I must reaffirm the difference between design and structure. The first concern of composers—and I mean not prehistoric musicians or Babylonians or Greeks but Western European composers in the musical tradition of which we ourselves are the heirs—was not to design music but to construct music. Their problem was, having made one sound, one phrase, to know what to do next. It was as simple—and as appallingly difficult—as that. Only through constructing music did they come upon the possibility of creating what the memory, but only the memory, enables the ear to apprehend as a musical design. And that process of construction generating design was not merely primitive; it has continued. As I shall try to show later, fugue is anyhow a matter of structure rather than of design, while sonata-form is a kind of design that was evolved in the process of finding the solution to certain problems of musical construction. One might go further and say that particularly since the decline of key-feeling, sonata-form has become little more than a time-convention rather like the painter's rectangular space-convention; but there again to begin to draw a parallel between music and painting is to begin confusion.

Let us get back to first principles, to the musician as he begins to 'compose': that is, to 'put music together', to construct it. It is improbable that he will begin with a single sound; he is more likely to begin with a melodic phrase or at the very least with a 'motive', a two- or three- or four-note germ. He has eternity in front of him, or as much of it as he wants to take, or dare inflict on the human ear (and human mind and memory) without over-tiring it. (I suppose the only

3

composers who have to fill a *definite* time are those who write for the films.) Even if he has words to set, they impose only a very elastic limit on him; he does not necessarily begin at their beginning, go straight through to their end, and then stop; he may do that, but we need only think of the first Handel aria that comes into our head to realize how very stretchable that elastic limit can be. Nowadays, when the art of music is no longer in its youth, the composer is helped by the existence of generally accepted conventions; if he is setting out to write an overture he knows that several generations of composers have proved that a good length for an overture is ten to twelve minutes, that nowadays a symphony may last for as long as an hour though half that time was long enough for the great classical symphonists, that an opera must provide a good evening's-money's-worth of entertainment but not more than that if it is not to risk cutting by the management nor less without risk of being paired unsuitably with some other short opera. And of course this same accumulated experience of his predecessors not only guides him as to suitable length; it provides him with all sorts of useful models for design. If he sets out to write a symphony, he can model it on the symphonies of Haydn or of Mahler or of Sibelius; he can take hints from all three and dozens of others, or he can reject them all—in which case he still has something definite to reject, a norm or series of norms from which to deviate. But how were these lengths arrived at? How did these models evolve?

We must never lose sight of our ideal musician who has just conceived a single musical thought and is facing the problem of how to go on, for this matter of 'going on' is the very heart of the business of musical composition. It is the problem of Walton and Britten, Shostakovich and Messiaen, as much as it was the problem of Tubal Cain; they have the advantage of knowing how thousands of other people have solved it but they still have to solve it for themselves, and the principles of solution remain unchanged. Having said something in music, if you want to go on you must do one of two things: you can say it again (either exactly the same or altered in some respect) or you can say something different. Now there is no harm in repeating something exactly in music, for music is not like speech in having a thought-content which becomes intolerable when repeated. (When a poet repeats a phrase, or a line like a ballad-refrain, he is taking advantage of the *musical* quality of words, e.g. 'answer, echoes, dying, dying, dying'; in fact the repeated words are often nonsense—'Hey nonny nonny', 'Binnorie, O Binnorie! ... By the bonnie milldams o' Binnorie.') In speech it is only the yokel who says everything twice over, but in music we are accustomed to such repetitions not only in yokels' music and in the composers who have come under its direct influence but in the work of the most highly cultivated musicians. Music exists for its own sake, not to convey a non-musical 'meaning'; if we try to fit such a meaning on to music, exact repetition will make the meaning ridiculous but not the music; that was demonstrated by the humorist who tried to make fun of the repeat of the exposition in the first movement of the Pastoral Symphony—'Beethoven he get up and he shave and he look out of the window and say "What a lovely day!"

I vill go in de country." Beethoven he get up and he shave and . . .' In music you can repeat anything, from a motive (as at the beginning of Beethoven's E flat Piano Sonata, Op. 31, No. 3), to a complete symphonic exposition—provided your motive is pregnant enough or your exposition interesting or beautiful enough. But obviously you cannot go on repeating even the loveliest motive or phrase even with minor alterations; you have really only postponed the solution of the problem. You must now say something else.

What is 'something else' musically? It may be just another melodic phrase. In the case of the Beethoven Sonata I have just mentioned, it is another motive: a two-bar one. But think of the vast range of particulars in which music can be 'the same' or 'different'! Think of only one aspect: melody. A melodic phrase can differ from another in length, in pitch, in key, in rhythm; it can closely resemble it in general outline, yet have different intervals (big upward leaps instead of little ones or *vice versa*); it can be different in dynamics (loud instead of soft). But music is not often melody only; it is harmony, texture, possibly scoring as well. Even precisely the same motive or melodic phrase may be harmonized differently, given a different accompanying texture, different scoring. But if all this seems to multiply bewilderingly the number of 'other things' a composer can say next, it does help him wonderfully to say the same thing in a different way. And that is the means by which he makes his musical structure cohere.

To keep saying the same thing, however beautiful, in the same way would quickly become intolerably

6

monotonous. On the other hand, to keep saying entirely different things would be incoherent. Broadly speaking, musicians have solved the problem in two different ways. One is to keep saying different things but always referring back between them to the first thing or to one central thing. In the very beginnings of our recorded Western European music, in plainsong, we find this recurrence of definite melodic patterns and the principle of the refrain; refrain is common in folk-song too. The same principle of saying something, saying something different, and then saying the first thing again and always referring back to it (or to some other principal topic) no matter how many other topics you may start, is also the principle of the *da capo* aria of Handel, the minuet-trio-minuet of the classics (both ABA forms) and the classical rondo (in its most primitive form ABACA). That is one solution; rather a mechanical solution but a perfectly good one. The other is organic, much more interesting and much more difficult to explain. It is the method of saying something that, while having enough features in common with the previous idea to be recognized as belonging to it, is nevertheless different. That method, too, comes from the very early days of Western European music and it has perhaps reached its highest organic development so far in the string quartets of Bartók and the symphonies of Sibelius, but there is no more convenient illustration of it than 'God save the King', a melody so familiar even to the nearly-tone-deaf that I can make my points without using music-type. 'God save our gracious King': that is, musically, the first 'thing said'. And how does the composer, whoever he was (and only

7

God and Dr. Scholes know), go on? By saying the same thing again rather differently: at a different pitch—'Long live our' is a third higher than 'God save our'—and with 'noble King' going down where 'gracious King' goes up; but recognizably the same phrase, exactly the same rhythmically and in length and nearly the same melodically. The clinching phrase 'God save the King' also recognizably belongs to them, not only because it is like them in 3/4 time and in the same key but because of the small intervals of the melody; 'God save the', in fact, is 'noble King' a tone lower and with the rhythm slightly altered. And so with the second half of the tune: 'Send him victorious' is rhythmically identical with 'God save our gracious King' and 'Long live our noble King' and has points of melodic identity —the repeated notes on 'God save', 'Long live' and 'Send him', and between 'noble King' and '-torious' —and 'Happy and glorious' repeats 'Send him victorious' a tone lower. 'Long to reign over us' is simply an ornamentation or 'variation' of the same rhythmic-melodic pattern, and the final 'God save the King' exactly balances the intermediate one. We may put it that the whole of 'God save the King' is organically developed from the first two bars: 'God save our gracious King'.

But it is seldom possible to develop a little two-bar germ in this way for any great length of time. However ingeniously the composer may modify and ornament it, it is bound to produce a feeling of monotony after a while. Its sense of *unity* will be magnificent, but unity without variety—more variety than can be got from modification and ornamentation of such a short theme—soon becomes very boring. At some

8

point, probably sooner rather than later, the composer will feel driven to say 'something else'; and having said it, and thus broken the close coherence of his texture, he will in some way use the other method, of harking back to the thing first said, to knit it up again. In actual fact nearly all our music is constructed by a combination of those two principles, which I have called the 'organic' and the 'mechanical'. (I call them that because of the effects they produce: one of natural growth, the other of contrivance. But I must remind you that the method of organic growth can be, and often is, imitated by academic manufacturers of music as well as by genuine creators; and that the great creators of the past never disdained the method of mechanical repetition.) Let me illustrate the combination by the beginning of the Beethoven E flat Piano Sonata (Op. 31, No. 3) to which I have already referred.

Beethoven begins with the tersest of possible remarks: a single motive. He repeats it exactly (bar 2) and then says something quite different (bars 3-4). Quite different yet not unrelated, for the first of the two harmonies that make up this second remark is the same as that which underlies bars 1 and 2. And then? Well, it is obvious enough that bars 5-6 are nothing but 3-4 with the melody—such as it is (let us think of it rather as the 'top' of the chords)—a semitone higher and with the harmonies changed. It may not be quite so obvious that bars 7-8 are also essentially the same; nevertheless they are. What does the idea of bars 3-4, repeated in bars 5-6, consist of? A thrice-repeated chord in the first of each pair of bars resolving on to a different chord in each second bar. And that is precisely what 7 and 8 consist of, too; the difference is that the 'top' of the chords in bar 7 has flowered melodically (a perfect illustration of what musicians mean by 'variation') and that the chord in bar 8, instead of being held for three beats like its counterparts in bars 4 and 6, is cut short by a third, totally different idea: a turn and an upward run of triplets—apparently quite disconnected and irrelevant, though very soon (bars 25 and 27) Beethoven will show you that he does not regard them as irrelevant. After which comes a repeat—a 'mechanical' repeat—of bars 1–7, exact so far as melody and harmony are concerned but completely altered in register and lay-out of the chords: yet another means of saying the same thing in a different way, the pianoforte equivalent of different scoring.

And so you can easily continue tracing Beethoven's method in this sonata movement of constructing a coherent musical texture, now by repeating some simple statement—with or without changes of the most varied kinds—now by throwing in a fresh idea and skilfully welding it to the earlier ones. That is his solution of the problem of going on, the composer's first problem. In some earlier periods of musical history composers, particularly composers of instrumental music, were well enough satisfied with their various solutions of that problem alone; to have found a method of constructing continuous musical texture seemed a sufficient achievement. The conception of having a *design* for that texture came later.

II

FUGUE AND SOME RELATED METHODS

I AM not sure whether all authorities would admit that fugue has any place in a discussion of musical design. As I myself expressed it on a previous page— unconsciously paraphrasing a remark of Tovey's— 'fugue is a matter of structure *rather than* of design' and the more closely your conception of musical design is based on design in the visual arts the more likely you are to feel that fugue is a style or a texture rather than a design. But I began with a warning that these parallels with the other arts are dangerously misleading and I now put forward the paradox that, while 'fugue'—in the abstract—has no special form, a good, well-knit fugue may be one of the finest types of purely musical design yet conceived by the mind of man. But design depends on *quality* of structure in a fugue; an ill-constructed fugue will be shapeless where-as a badly constructed sonata-form movement will at least have a recognizable shape, however deformed. The design of a fugue is purely musical; it is conceivable only in time, with none of the spatial analogies that are bound to creep into one's conception of sonata-form unless one closes one's mind against them very firmly indeed; it arises purely out of musical structure. A well-constructed fugue is *ipso facto* a well-designed fugue, if nothing else; it may not necessarily be good, living music. But an ill-constructed fugue can have no design and cannot fail to be bad music.

The history of the evolution of the fugue is one of

the most instructive of all facets of musical history, for it brilliantly illustrates how the problem of constructing music, of going on when you have once started, leads to the creation of texture and then of design.

The very beginnings of texture are so primitive that we may consider them as 'natural' rather than a matter of conscious art: the drone, the 'polyphony' produced when, of a number of people who try to sing the same tune, one or two unhappy creatures manage—perhaps unaware of their own limitation—to emit only repetitions of the same note, or (at best) part company with their fellows and rejoin them only at the end of the phrase. The accident happens every Sunday in some church or other to this day; it was equally familiar a thousand years ago and in other lands than ours. For the next step, a deliberate polyphony based on this kind of accident, may be found in Russian folk-music of the last century and in the earliest form of non-single-line music known to Western European culture: the organum. Organum is usually defined simply as the singing of a Gregorian melody in parallel fifths or fourths, but the very earliest clear and reliable account of organum—the tenth-century treatise *Musica Enchiriadis*—describes not only this strict parallel type but a freer type in which the two voices begin in unison, open out into parallel fourths (our still familiar accident), and return to unison at the end of the phrase. And it seems pretty obvious that this 'free organum' was the earlier form.

That accident and its legalization by the early-medieval theorists marked the beginning (so far as Western art-music is concerned) of harmony, counterpoint, texture. Tenth-century musicians, however, only realized at first that two different notes sounded together, if they were the right notes, sounded pleasant. Further steps were soon taken. Mainly parallel motion, with oblique motion at beginnings and ends, was varied by contrary motion of the two parts. Then —tremendously important—two or three notes in one part were sung against a single note in the other, instead of simple note-against-note. . . . I do not propose to offer a potted history of the evolution of polyphonic forms during the Middle Ages. (Potted history can hardly help being misleading history.) But the intelligent reader should be able to guess for himself the inevitable lines of development: the addition of a third voice to the original two, the flowering out of more and more notes in the added part or parts to each note of the basic plainsong. Both these developments are essentially developments of texture but the second of them led directly—after a due interval of time—to a structural device that has been used in one form or another ever since, right up to the present day: a most striking example of the way in which musical texture is liable to generate musical structure, just as musical structure is capable of producing from its own inner laws what we recognize as musical design. To condense several centuries of technical evolution into a couple of sentences, what happened was this: from the adding of a second or third or fourth part of a more florid nature to the original plainsong of the tenor (so-called originally because it *held on* to the basic melody) it was an easy step, though slowly, imperceptibly taken, to the use of the basic plainsong in ever longer notes as the backbone of a whole protracted polyphonic composition.

I have said that the problem of 'going on' is 'the very heart of the business of composition'. Even the church composers of the Dark Ages had solved some of the problems of 'going on' in a single musical line and actually solved them in the direction of the principles I sketched in the latter part of Chapter 1. The discovery or invention of organum, the rude beginning of polyphony, led at first only to a thickening out of that single musical line; it was texture, not structure; the early polyphonic composers had no idea how to 'go on' with their polyphonic fabric except as a thickened out, embellished single line. The plainsong backbone first gave them an idea. Set down your basic melody in fairly long notes of equal value—and compose a polyphonic texture round it. It is at once obvious what possibilities are opened. In terms of a modern tune: if you have conceived the melody of 'God save the King'—well, you have just a fourteen-bar tune. Add other parts above or below it: you have only enriched its texture, harmonized it. You still have only your fourteen bars. But add more florid parts, so florid that to get in their six or eight or more notes to each note of the tune you have to sing the tune itself more slowly; you arrive at the idea of writing out the tune in long notes, each lasting a whole bar, and composing florid parts all round it. And when you have written out 'God save the King' in whole-bar notes, you will find it stretches to forty bars instead of fourteen. More: if you want to construct an eighty-bar piece, all you have to do is to write it out again and compose different florid parts round it. The medieval composer would in this way compose a whole Mass round the thread of a single melody, generally a plain-

14

song melody but often a popular, secular tune. The same structural principle was carried on into many of the instrumental 'fantasies' of the Elizabethan period and—the fundamental melody in the bass instead of the tenor and itself grown livelier and more interesting —into the later 'air on a ground bass' and 'chaconne'.[1] It is the structural principle of Purcell's 'When I am laid in earth', of the Crucifixus of Bach's B minor Mass, of the finale of Brahms's Haydn Variations and of the last movement of his E minor Symphony, of the passacaglia interludes in Shostakovich's *Lady Macbeth of Mtsensk* and Britten's *Peter Grimes*.

I say 'the structural principle is the same': Purcell and Brahms and Shostakovich and Britten write out their 'given' tune a number of times and then compose around and above it. But there are of course many differences from medieval practice besides the increased rhythmic interest of the basic melody and the fact that it became generally not only basic but the bass: the most important is that the basic melody is specially written for its purpose and is *much shorter*— usually not more than eight bars. Length of composition is obtained by repeating the basic theme instead of having it very long. The Gregorian melody or popular song written out in long notes really ceased to have a profile of its own; it served as a backbone, a series of given notes, but a series of notes written down at random might have served the composer almost as well. The complex of parts written round it is apt to sound straggling, *design*less. The shorter basic theme is more recognizable from its stronger

---

[1] I do not forget that the short repeated ground bass is itself as old as 'Sumer is icumen in'.

melodic and rhythmic profile, and its constant repetitions impose a recognizable design on the music built round it. (Of course other factors play a part in the design of the Bachian and post-Bachian chaconne—modern conceptions of harmony and symmetrical phrasing—but the one I have mentioned seems the most vital.)

That is one kind of musical design that grew out of this structural device. But it is less important than another kind, which arose from the feeling that something might be done to relate the different voice-parts to each other. So far as one can see, the first step in this direction was exchange of parts: one voice would sing phrase X, a second phrase Y—both X and Y being free florid parts added to perhaps one note of the basic plainsong—and then repeat but with parts exchanged, the first voice singing Y, the second X. Perhaps from this came the discovery of 'imitation'. If one part sings XY, while a second sings YX, each seems to imitate the other and the next step of making the imitation closer, so that the second part begins X before the first has finished it, would suggest itself to any lively mind. Or, of course, this sort of close imitation may have been hit upon simply by accident just as the very beginnings of polyphony may have been. If several voices set out to sing the same tune and one sings the wrong notes in the right place, you get crude polyphony; but if the odd man out sings the right notes in the wrong place, beginning too soon or too late, you get crude imitation. However discovered, imitation between voices was soon found to be valuable. Here was a means of *weaving* texture. Instead of loose straggling threads of melody lying side by side,

16

related to each other and to a basic theme only in so far that they sounded well together, the different threads could now be really related—usually by modelling the opening of a phrase in one part on the opening of a phrase, heard just before, in another part. The imitation might be exact, the second voice (say) dropping a minor third and then rising a semitone and so on just like the first voice, or it might be freer: the second voice rising and falling in similar but not always identical intervals. And it was not often found possible to carry the imitation very far. (When imitation was exact and carried out at length, it was said to be according to canon, to law: nowadays we simply call such a piece of imitation a 'canon'.) Medieval music abounds in various methods of constructing texture by means of imitation, sometimes in conjunction with other devices. For instance, two voice-parts may proceed in canon over a two-note rhythmical ground-bass played on some instrument. But by the end of the sixteenth century one particular kind of imitative structure had established its pre-eminence equally in vocal and in instrumental music.

One part starts alone; after a bar or two a second enters a fifth (or fourth) or octave higher or lower, singing or playing the same theme while the first voice continues freely; then a third part enters, and perhaps a fourth, always—or almost always—at that space of an octave or fifth from each other, each with the theme while the earlier voices now go their own way. (Why that spacing of octave and fifth? Because the principal types of human voice lie roughly a fifth or octave from each other. A melody that 'lies' comfortably for a tenor will be all right an octave higher for a soprano, while for a contralto or bass it will be more manageable a fourth or fifth higher or lower.) There is a first-rate way of constructing musical texture; if you have four voices you can weave a piece of music four times as long as your melodic theme and all tightly knit together *by* that theme. But when all your voices have entered and sung or played the theme, what do you do next to keep things going? To let all the voices then proceed freely is simply to unravel a texture that has begun by being well woven; it seems untidy. To let one or two parts take up the original theme again is only to postpone the difficulty. (It is the old, the original, problem of all musical composition: how to keep going.) The favourite solution of our own Elizabethans and their Continental contemporaries was to dovetail a new theme into the end of the texture woven from the first one—and repeat the process as many times as necessary. That is the constructive principle of many a madrigal for voices, many a fantasia for strings, many a ricercar for organ. In a vocal work each new theme generally coincides with a fresh line of text; the principle was probably discovered through vocal settings; but it is the same in both vocal and instrumental works of this type.

It was a type popular for a long period of musical history and many masterpieces were written in it. But an art like music progresses by exhausting forms and techniques, becoming dissatisfied with them, and finding new ones by eliminating or reacting against the weaknesses of the old ones. (Only let us beware of innocently concluding that technical progress is the same thing as higher aesthetic value; you may invent a more satisfactory type of design or a richer range of harmony, but you will not necessarily be able to compose lovelier music in them.) This method of constructing quite lengthy polyphonic fabrics by knitting a number of short passages each from a different theme, and weaving the beginning of each passage into the end of the previous one or joining them by a freer interlude, was open to the objection that it tended to straggle. If the various themes were too much alike, the effect was liable to be monotonous; if they were too sharply contrasted the whole would lack homogeneity. (Naturally one is less conscious of these difficulties in the best specimens of the type; every type has its special problems which only its masters can solve satisfactorily.) By Bach's time a new type of structure had been evolved: as structure looser, yet more satisfactory as design. It begins like the previous type but having completed its exposition of the first theme—that is, when the last of the individual parts has sung or played it—the composer takes a freer course.

The one thing he usually does not do is, like his predecessors, to invent a second theme like the first, equally important, and write an exposition of that too. He may introduce a second theme at this point (but if so it will generally be of secondary interest); he may continue with his first theme or with the countermelody played or sung by the first voice when the main theme passed from it to the second voice. The one thing he will almost certainly do at this point is to modulate, to change key. (Just what that implies is explained on a later page.) The sense of key, as we know it, was late in developing; it is, roughly, about four hundred years old—by no means an everlasting musical fact, as some people appear to suppose. But by Bach's time it was firmly established. Musicians were intensely conscious of key, conscious of wandering when they left the main key, conscious of 'reaching home' when they returned to it; much more conscious of it, I suspect, than we are nowadays. Key variety and key unity were powerful new tools for musical design. So the polyphonic composer of Bach's time, having stated his theme in all parts in the old manner, begins to get variety by modulating; he will probably get still more variety by introducing fresh material in the way of passage-work or subsidiary themes; and he will probably preserve unity by bringing in his original theme or counter-melody here and there, perhaps constantly, in fresh keys. When he wants to finish, he can give a due sense of finality by returning not only to the main theme but to the original key. When he does finish he will have written what we can all recognize as a *fugue*.

The actual term 'fugue' was used much earlier in musical history and originally meant no more than 'imitation' (the first voice being fugitive from the second); but when we talk of 'fugue' nowadays, we mean this sort of fugue, Bach's sort of fugue. Many other things that I have not mentioned may occur in a fugue, but they are not essential to it. The features I have described are the essential ones. They have all developed through striving to solve those three basic problems: how to create texture (thickness, more than just a single-line melody), how to continue weaving texture (in time), and how to give design or sense of direction to the weaving. The Bachian fugue is only one of the solutions—or one group of solutions—to those problems, but none has proved more satisfactory.

III

VARIATIONS

I HAVE already pointed out that one of the ways of 'going on' in music is to say something and then to say it again differently. Obviously it can then be said a third time, and a fourth, with more or other differences and so *ad infinitum*—or at any rate to the limit of human patience. As a musical *design* the result is exceedingly primitive—and remains primitive even in the hands of a Bach or a Brahms. (I suggest that, next to Beethoven, the composers who have most successfully developed it above the primitive are Haydn and César Franck.) Yet its very primitiveness is such a challenge to a composer's skill as a craftsman that every great instrumental composer for four hundred years has accepted the challenge. Consider for a moment what the problem is: to repeat what is *essentially* the same piece of music, usually quite a short piece, again and again and again not merely with differences but with differences that will constantly hold the listener's interest. Could there be a harder test of a composer's technical inventiveness? Indeed the test is so hard that variation-writing is one of the best exercises for the student-composer; any man who has learned to write interesting and really varied variations will have acquired a superb stock of technical devices which he will be able to use anywhere in his work when he wishes to make his texture more interesting than a mere hymn-tune-like affair of four-part-har-mony or melody-accompanied-by-block-chords. One might go so far as to say that any non-contrapuntal composition of any scope at all involves a certain amount of variation-technique, a composer constantly needs to vary a theme, to write perhaps just one varia-tion on it, without necessarily composing a whole set of variations.

What exactly is 'variation-technique'? How does one write variations? The methods have differed in different historical periods. The earliest way was ornamentation of the melody by grace-notes and so on. But variations are written not only on a tune but on a whole bit of texture: tune and bass and harmonic filling-in. The Elizabethan virginal composers, who loved to write variations on folk-songs and sometimes constructed very long works by this means, used to vary the bass, the counter-melodies and so on, as much as the melody. Illustration is a good deal easier than explanation; I have used 'God save the King' to make more than one point already and I now propose to take it, or what Beethoven did with it, to illustrate this one. Let us look, then, for a moment at Beet-hoven's set of seven variations for piano on this most familiar of tunes; the very familiarity of the tune will help us to hear it in its varied forms. It will suffice if we look only at the adventures of the first two bars. But I must begin by quoting the first two bars of the theme as Beethoven has written it, for, familiar as the melody may be, Beethoven's harmonization is not familiar and (as I have just remarked) variations are based not on the tune only but on everything else in the given theme, which in this case as usual includes the harmony. Here, then, are the first two bars of the theme:

And here are the two equivalent bars of the first variation:

Let us see precisely what Beethoven has done. Not really very much, yet the sum of the little details adds up to something decidedly different in character.

He has added only two little ornamental notes to the melody: the B that is the second quaver in bar 1 and the B that is the final quaver in bar 2. The real interest lies in the changes of texture: the first beat of bar 1 left unharmonized, the second harmonized with an A minor chord instead of the expected C major one, both bass and middle part slightly ornamented in the same way as the melody—the middle part in particular being given more movement, and its colour heightened by the F *sharp* in bar 2.

Variation II is not nearly such plain sailing: here are its first two bars:

Perhaps you do not recognize in it 'God save the King' at all. (It might be amusing to test it on somebody not in the secret: 'What familiar tune is buried here?') I doubt whether it would bring even the most patriotic audience to its feet. It might almost be the beginning of a Two-Part Invention by Bach. But the melody is still there, however disguised, its first three notes in the left hand and 'our gracious King' wreathed round with semiquavers in the right hand; it is marked with crosses. The implied harmony is the same—or, rather, the same as in Variation I (the chord on 'save' A minor instead of C major). And the bass of bar 2 is still recognizably only an ornamentation of the bass of the second bar of the theme. Two other things in Variation II have been suggested by Variation I, not by the theme itself: the semiquaver figure on 'God' is a further growth from the quaver C-B that opens the first variation, and the F sharp at the end of bar 1 obviously comes from the F sharp in the second bar of Variation I. The C sharp passing-note between C and D is yet another touch of colour. But the chief difference in this variation is in the general texture: two contrapuntal parts instead of the block chords of the theme or the slightly broken up chords of Variation I.

Now observe how a principle of design begins to assert itself even in such a loose structure as a string of variations. Variation I has been based on the theme, Variation II on Variation I—and has got some way from the theme. If Variation III in turn were developed out of the second variation, the theme might well be lost sight of altogether. Indeed that does happen quite often in the great classical sets of variations; only much study and careful listening reveal the relationship; but sooner or later in the great classical sets the composer will do what Beethoven does immediately here. (He is writing only seven variations, so everything is planned on a small scale.) He comes back to a variation whose relationship to the theme is easily recognizable. So Variation III, though quite unlike the theme in character, is yet obviously derived directly from it:

The melody is syncopated, literally 'jazzed', but there can be no doubt about it. The block chords of the accompanying harmony are broken into conventional left-hand semiquaver figuration of the period, but they are the original chords of Ex. 1, without the changes and the touches of colour of the two intervening variations. The only respect in which

Variation III is indebted to Variation I, and not the theme, is its first beat: unharmonized and not forgetting the B natural. Above all, in texture we have got back firmly to the feeling of 'tune with accompaniment', whereas in Variation I the bass and middle part had shown signs of coming to life on their own, and in Variation II the whole thing had almost resolved into a two-part invention.

There is no need to follow the rest of Beethoven's variations on 'God save the King' in detail. (It is as well to remember that we have been talking only about the first two bars of each variation, though the opening bars more or less give their stamp to the whole variation.) But the general plan is as follows:

Variation IV: repeated notes or chords flung about in different registers.

Variation V: in C *minor*, instead of major; a *con espressione* melody flowering out in triplet ornamentation, with an accompaniment of triplet broken chords. A distant ancestor, through Field's nocturnes, of Chopin's.

Variation VI: Major again, but the time-signature changed from 3/4 to 4/4. A brisk little *alla marcia*, chordal, rather in the style of the opera marches of the time.

Variation VII: Still 4/4; brilliant passage-work.

Coda: The brilliant passage-work dies down to a brief *adagio* in 3/4 time, strongly reminding one of the theme, with a strong flavour of D minor but cadencing into C major for a final display of *allegro* fireworks.

The important point is that there *is* a discernible plan, however loose; even in this quite unimportant little work, Beethoven does not just allow one variation to follow another. I do not say that it would be impossible to alter the order without serious detriment to the whole set, yet Variation II had to come *after* Variation I, we have seen how Variation III is placed just right, Variations V and VI bring changes of mode and time-signature just when one is beginning to get tired of C major and 3/4 time, and the brilliant finale could come nowhere else. Indeed the plan not only exists but may be said to conform to something not unlike a formula for sets of variations at this period: the turning of the theme into a march (sometimes a minuet), the slow variation or the variation in the minor, or both in one as here, just before the end as a foil to the brilliant finale, the interruption of the finale itself by a few slow bars or a pause or some similar effect—all these were popular features of the variation-sets of the Viennese classical period. One of them—the slow variation just before the final fire-works—appears in the great set of variations that forms the finale of the 'Eroica' Symphony.

The 'Eroica' variations are, of course, enormously different both in scale and in artistic value from this little set on 'God save the King'—though, as it happens, the latter were published in 1804, the 'Eroica' year. But they are different in kind as well as in degree. They are, among other things, an attempt to make variations *symphonic*, to make a connected organism out of what had hitherto generally been a succession—albeit often a carefully planned succession—of organisms. We—and by 'we' I mean all but a very few specialists—know very little of the enormous symphonic literature that is the real background of Haydn's and Mozart's works; it would be foolhardy to assert that Haydn was 'the first' to do anything at all. But broadly speaking it is true to say that Haydn was the earliest known master to break away successfully from the simple chain-of-variations. (I do not forget the wonderful planning of Bach's 'Goldberg' set, with the interspersed canons as milestones, but the set remains a chain—however splendid as such.) It was Haydn, particularly in the slow movements of his last symphonies, who was the first to 'cross' variations with other types of structure, such as the rondo, to interrupt them with free dramatic interpolations, to write variations on two alternating themes. For it was from Haydn that Beethoven borrowed the design of the wonderful slow movement of his Ninth Symphony:

First theme: B flat, 4/4 time, *adagio*.

Second theme: D major, 3/4 time, *andante moderato*.

Variation I on first theme: B flat.

Variation I on second theme: G major.

Variation II on first theme: E flat and C flat.

Variation III on first theme: B flat.

Coda: B flat

—a design which he repeated almost exactly in the slow movement, the famous 'Convalescent's Hymn of Thanksgiving', of the A minor String Quartet.

As for the finale of the Choral Symphony, it is a classical example of the fusion of variation-form with rondo and fugue and Heaven knows what beside.

But the 'Eroica' finale is a 'neater' example of symphonic handling of the variation form, arguably a finer example, and indisputably an easier example to discuss in limited space. In the ordinary 'set of variations' we are accustomed to hear the theme first. In this case we do not. Those first eleven bars culminating in *tutti* chords are certainly not the theme; they are only introductory. And when the strings begin pizzicato, is that the theme? It is certainly the *melody*; but we hear two variations on it and then in the third variation it passes to the bass while the oboe in the treble plays against it the tune we generally consider the real theme of the variations. . . . And there, by the way, is a first-rate instance of the danger of trying to lay down the law on some points of musical analysis. You may say that the bass is the real theme, that the oboe tune is only an important counter-melody (which disappears again in Variation IV); or you may say that everything before the appearance of the oboe theme is only elaborate introduction, and point for confirmation to the piano variations on the same theme which Beethoven had written a year or two before where he calls the parallel passage 'Introduzione col basso del tema'. In neither case will you be wrong; musical analysis often allows two equally good interpretations of the same facts. However, that is a digression. What matters is that Beethoven is writing, not variations mainly on a melody as Handel does in his so-called 'Harmonious Blacksmith' set or mainly on a bass like Bach in the 'Goldberg' set (which is essentially a vast and glorified specimen of the chaconne or variations-on-a-ground-bass type mentioned in the previous chapter), but variations on an idea that is both tune and bass. And instead of each variation coming to an end defined by a well-marked cadence and perhaps a pause, most of them run in to the next more or less without breaks. (There are cadences, which are the musical equivalents of punctuation marks, but they are not left exposed and obvious.) One of the most interesting of the many points of comparison between the 'Eroica' finale and the piano variations on the same theme is the much greater continuity of the orchestral variations. Among other devices, Beethoven dovetails in little bridge-passages of perhaps six to twelve bars covering the transition from one variation to the next.

Thus once again from a simple, a most primitive device for constructing music, mere repetition with changes, it has proved possible for a master to evolve a real musical organism which certainly has a satisfactory shape in the time sense though, like a fugue, it is lacking in almost all the 'balancing' elements that we connect with design in the spatial sense. (It does not lack all 'balancing' elements; the two fugal variations in the 'Eroica' finale in a sense correspond to each other; spatial concepts always creep in somewhere— but they are inessential to satisfactory musical design.)

The variation form since Beethoven has developed on three main lines, which may with rough justice be called the Brahmsian, the Tchaikovskian and the Franckian. The Brahmsian and Tchaikovskian both derive from Beethoven through Schumann. Both lay more stress on the individual variations than on the composition as a whole; the satisfaction given by a whole set of variations by Brahms or Tchaikovsky is only the satisfaction of hearing a well arranged and contrasted and built-up sequence of individual units. Brahms's 'Paganini' Variations are two 'works'; he never intended both sets to be played together. His mastery as a variation-writer—and I suppose he was the greatest since Beethoven—lies in what one can only call his superb 'technical imagination', his fertility in embroidering new and beautiful patterns over the basic theme. Tchaikovsky also concentrates on the individual variation but he does not so much work out the inner possibilities of the theme as twist the theme itself into new shapes—really a much easier proceeding. And although that is something profoundly different from the great classical method of variation-writing continued by Brahms, it has precedents in the classical variation: the march that is the sixth of Beethoven's 'God save the King' set and the various other minuets and marches that turn up in classical variations generally. But whereas the classical masters would include only one, or perhaps two, little genre pieces of this kind in a set of variations, Tchaikovsky tends to make his sets little or nothing but *transformations*, rather than true variations, of the theme: waltzes, chorales, mazurkas, polonaises. And he has found numerous followers, including Elgar ('Enigma') and Britten ('Variations on a Theme by Frank Bridge').

Franck's method is different again. Like Tchaikovsky, he is happier in transforming a theme than in varying it in the classical way. But he considers the whole rather than the parts. No one has done more than he to develop the Haydn-Beethoven conception of the symphonic treatment of variations, by crossing them with other structural devices. Consider the set for piano and orchestra that he actually called 'symphonic'. The first fifteen pages (of the Eulenburg score) are an introduction, in which the theme and certain points in the variations are foreshadowed; the theme proper appears on page 15; and after the six variations comes an enormous thirty-page finale largely based on a transformation of the chief theme of the introduction. From that it was no great step to the 'programme' variations of Franck's pupil d'Indy (*Istar*) and Strauss's *Don Quixote*, in which the adventures of the theme or themes correspond to episodes in a story.

IV

THE SONATA PRINCIPLE

ONE very important way of 'saying something differently' in music—a way that hitherto I have not touched on, or touched only in passing—is to say it in another key. By repeating a phrase or a longer stretch of music in a fresh key, you obviously do not make the slightest change in its identity, its recognizability; but it is obviously repetition-with-a-difference—and a difference of something other than mere pitch. As a matter of fact you can, and composers often do, repeat a phrase at a higher or lower pitch without going into another key. Here, for instance, is the first phrase of 'God save the King' with a repetition a third higher but still in the key of G major:

Repetition a tone higher was a favourite device of Beethoven's for getting up melodic steam at the outset of a movement and one could imagine him continuing the above by starting a third repetition a third or a tone higher still and then breaking off after the first bar of the theme into scales or other passage-work, leading up to a forte, *tutti*, re-statement of the theme an octave higher than its first appearance. One might have all this without leaving the original key. But if, instead of repeating the first two bars as in the previous example, one repeats them like this:

something else has happened. They have not merely been lifted in pitch, they have been lifted on to another plane or, as we say, into another key (in this case, B major). In actual composition the transition to a new key may happen quite suddenly like this, in which case it will probably sound rather dramatic, rather a wrench, or it may be contrived gradually—the more usual way—even almost imperceptibly: the difference between a step and a slope. But however it happens you will, if you are really musical, feel a little uncomfortable if the music does not return to the key it started in (or at least to the major form of the key if it started in the minor, and *vice versa*).

Our feeling for key nowadays has unquestionably been gradually and progressively weakened first by the nineteenth-century chromaticism of Chopin, Wagner and others which began by *expanding* key (but key is like elastic, in that the more you expand it the thinner and weaker it becomes), then by Debussyan harmony and still more modern forms of harmony which began by taking even less account of key and went on by trying deliberately to get rid of it altogether on the ground that it was a 'fetter'. (Whether the 'atonal', the no-key composers are right in considering key a hampering limitation is a point to which I shall return later.) I doubt whether even the most conservative musician of to-day is as strongly key-conscious as any musician of the eighteenth and early nineteenth centuries. But unless we possess some feeling for key, some instinctive perception that things which are in the same key are happening on the same plane and that things in more or less distant keys (very roughly: the more nearly the same number of flats or sharps in two keys, the 'closer' they are to each other) are happening on more or less distant planes, unless we feel this we do not perceive what it is no exaggeration to call the mainspring of music during the great classical period of Haydn, Mozart, Beethoven and Schubert and for a good long time before and after. Lacking it, we shall listen to their music as a young child might read an adult novel: enjoying a series of incidents but finding the love-interest (which is the main-spring of most novels) completely meaningless. There are plenty of people who listen to music in that ingenuous way and who get a lot of pleasure from doing so, but they miss a great deal of the real point of the music, its inner tensions, its real drama.

The most important of all types of musical design, what we call 'sonata-form' or 'first-movement form', the broad design that in some way or another underlies the first movements of the vast majority of symphonies and sonatas (to say nothing of a great many slow movements and final movements, or of a large number of overtures and the like), really makes sense only in terms of key. Some people seem to believe that its sense lies in a sort of drama or conflict with first and second 'subjects' as protagonists; they will even tell you that the 'first subject' is or ought to be equivalent to the masculine element, the 'second' to the feminine.

Now that may be partially true of some movements in sonata-form but is certainly not true of sonata-form in general. Substitute 'key' for 'subject' and you come at least *nearer* the truth. . . . But first of all let us see how key begins to be a principle of design.

One of the simplest ways of bringing variety into a simple hymn-tune or popular melody without introducing a new melodic element into the short space available is to modulate, that is, to go into a new key part way through. The most natural key to choose is what we call 'the dominant': talking (for the sake of simplicity of explanation) in terms of major keys only, the dominant is the key with one more sharp or one less flat than the main, the 'tonic', key; its keynote is always a fifth higher than the original keynote. If the tonic is C, the dominant is G, and so on. Now one of the mysterious inner laws of music, its real law of gravity (too subtle to explain here), is the tendency of basses in harmony, and of keys, to fall a perfect fifth; to modulate into a sharper key is to have a feeling equivalent to lifting or pushing uphill, to go into a flatter one is, roughly, to allow gravity to have its way. When the tune has made its little effort and modulated into the dominant key therefore, on to what we may call the next 'higher' plane, it will tend to slip back very easily and naturally to the original plane of the tonic key to finish up. (I repeat: unless it returns to the original key-plane at the end, a composition will sound to anyone with a sense of key unsatisfactory and unfinished —unless of course it is such a long composition, so harmonically complicated or so bold in intermediate modulations that the original key has been washed out of one's memory.) The modulation may not be to the

36

dominant, of course; that is only the nearest, most natural key to go to. The subdominant key (i.e., the one a fifth *lower*, with one *less* sharp or one *more* flat) is equally near, but to go into it is simply to follow the law of gravity and every student-composer knows that it is much easier to go into the subdominant than to climb back out of it convincingly; in fact if you go first into the subdominant, your tune will very likely not sound satisfactory at all if you merely return to the home-key direct; you may have to go back by a round-about route, perhaps through the dominant.

That very simple principle of getting variety-within-unity by modulating and then returning to the home-key became, as the result of a long process of evolution, the principle of sonata-form. I cannot describe that process here; I must telescope it. Or, rather, I will describe one intermediate stage which flourished in the early part of the eighteenth century. The composer constructs a fair length of musical texture of which the first part is in the tonic key, the latter part in the dominant (he then repeats it); he doubles its length and brings the whole thing back to the key-plane on which it started by re-writing what is substantially the same music but now with the first part in the dominant and the second in the tonic (and then repeats that, too). A good many of the movements of Bach's keyboard suites are constructed on that pattern, which, like most patterns for instrumental music, was originally a constructional device for making a little go a long way. Now it was a very natural thing for a composer to mark the appearance of the dominant key in the first half, and consequently of the tonic key in the second half, by giving his material a new twist or even by introducing new material, a new theme. When he did that he had already evolved an early type of sonata-form:

> First subject in tonic
> Second subject in dominant
> (and repeat)
> First subject in dominant
> Second subject in tonic
> (and repeat).

And here let me observe that 'subject' does not mean 'theme', though careless writers use the two words as if they were synonymous. A theme is a single idea, a sentence, if you like; a 'subject' in a sonata or symphony is at least a paragraph, consisting probably of several appearances of the 'theme', or even of several themes or subsidiary ideas hardly definite enough to be called themes.

The next historical step in the growth of sonata-form was to introduce further key-contrast between the main halves of the movement, between 'second subject in dominant' and 'first subject in dominant'— obviously to break up the over-long stretch of dominant key in the middle. Here for a short passage, at first a very short one, composers would go into remoter keys before returning to the first subject; and, having got further key-contrast in this way and feeling that the tonic key tended to be lost sight of if its return were so long delayed, they would now bring back the first subject, too, in the tonic. Thus they arrived at modern sonata-form which at its most primitive is simply:

First subject in tonic
Second subject in dominant
                    (repeated)
Passage in remoter keys
First subject in tonic
Second subject in tonic
                    (repeated).

There are several points to be noted in this. The most important is the 'passage in remoter keys'. At first it was no more than that: a free, modulatory, almost improvisatory interlude. But it was very natural to construct it partly or even wholly out of previous themes and, as they tended to get treated here in fresh ways as well as in fresh keys, people talked of 'developing' them and this section became known as the 'development'. Nevertheless, I must repeat: its basic function was to provide strong key-contrast, not to 'develop' themes. Another point is that the second repeat, of the 'development' and the recapitulation of both subjects in the tonic, was abandoned long before the repeat of what we call the 'exposition' (first subject in tonic, second in dominant or other contrasting key), though one still finds it in some mature Beethoven. A third point very well worth making—it emphasizes that 'theme' and 'subject' are not in the least synonymous—is that even in the more modern type of sonata-form the second main key (dominant or whatever it may be) is not *necessarily* signalized by the appearance of new material; there are still a number of cases in Haydn where the 'second subject' (i.e., the passage in the dominant key) is based on the same *theme* as the 'first subject'; the first movement of

39

Mozart's 'Haffner' Symphony is another instance, the first movement of Schumann's Piano Concerto yet another. (Try to analyse the Schumann in terms of theme and you will get nowhere; analyse it in terms of key and everything becomes clear at once.)

The outline of classical sonata-form given above shows it, as I said, at its most primitive. It soon grew appendages. Being usually a quick movement, it was sometimes introduced by a slow passage that might or might not be thematically connected with it; Haydn's 'Drum-roll' Symphony has a slow introduction that *is* thematically connected but in the majority of cases the slow introduction is rather in the nature of 'chairman's remarks' and has just about as much bearing on the principal matter in hand as such remarks commonly have. In Beethoven's Seventh Symphony, on the other hand, the slow introduction has grown to the dimensions and interest almost of an independent movement without, however, losing its sense of being an introduction. An appendage at the other end was the coda (literally, 'tail'). Just as the second subject in the exposition was commonly rounded off with the musical equivalent of lines and flourishes, the codetta (or 'little tail'), so the whole movement was rounded off even more decidedly by a passage which in the hands of the mature Haydn and the young Beethoven became something like a second 'development', sometimes as long as the first one.

But the really important evolutionary steps in sonata-form are those which have turned that bare scheme into a potentially living organism. Broadly speaking, they are the tendencies—most strongly developed in later Beethoven and in Brahms—to make every part of the movement more thematic and to cover up the joins. In the early days of classical sonata-form the passages of transition from one subject to another, one key to another, were apt to be perfunctory: effected by scales and empty, or at least non-thematic, passage-work; it never occurred to the composers that joins were features to be concealed. It did occur to later composers; they make their transitional passages more and more from bits of actual thematic material; they use all their technical craft to embroider over cadences and to produce at least the semblance of continuously woven texture, not of pieces of material sewn together. That is the normal course of the historical development of an art-form. But let me drop in here a parenthetic note of warning: we must not assume that historical development and technical progress necessarily heighten aesthetic value. A sonata movement in which every transition, every bar, is thematic is not *ipso facto* better than one in which all the seams show. The modern well-woven work may be the product of skilled but uninspired craftsmanship; the one with the seams showing may yet have beautifully made seams and the whole thing may be inspired by the breath of creative genius. Such differences are matters of aesthetic fashion: sometimes we delight in clear sun-lit form, at other times we try to conceal it.

Two other steps were taken at a very early stage in this history of sonata-form: the second 'subject' was liable very early to be composed of several 'themes' and the first subject eventually followed its example, with the result that in the later stages of the romantic symphony one finds first movements based on whole big groups of themes. And the key-pattern too became more complex. That is, inwardly complex within the general pattern of 'first and second subject in two contrasting keys—development in remoter keys—first and second subjects in the same key'. When we say that a symphony is in C minor we never mean that every movement is in C minor (though in Bach's and Handel's day a suite in D usually had every movement in D); only the first movement and the scherzo may be in C minor, the slow movement in A flat major, the trio of the scherzo and the finale in C major. And even the first movement, being in sonata-form, will not be wholly in C minor; we only mean that C minor is its main key, its home key, its tonic; even that may end in C major, for C minor and C major are on what I have called the same key-plane. (Technically, we say that they are 'different modes of the same key'.) Similarly a 'subject' in C minor will probably not stay in C minor the whole time; there will occur passing modulations, perhaps even to relatively remote keys (a tendency more and more marked as we get later in history), but C minor—or whatever it is—will be the predominating key of the subject.

Now one of the chief values in art of a ready-conceived form like this is that the skilled artist can play a very subtle game for the benefit of those who, like himself, understand the rules. Knowing that all his intelligent listeners will expect him to go into a certain key, he can amuse them by going into another one—or by threatening or pretending to go into another one, or by approaching the expected key by an unusual route, perhaps roundabout, perhaps a startling short cut. He may, as Haydn loves to do, return to the opening theme in the tonic key quite early in the development as if he were going to recapitulate, and then dart off again before he decides to come to the true recapitulation (but the listener will not appreciate the point unless he recognizes the tonic key as well as the theme itself). He may, as Beethoven does in the first movement of the 'Eroica', return to the tonic key at the beginning of the recapitulation only to modulate again suddenly into remote key-regions for a while. The recapitulation that merely repeats the exposition with the minimum of alterations needed to get the second subject into the tonic key is rare, and is apt to seem very perfunctory. Haydn and Mozart, to say nothing of Beethoven, often show their genius at its finest in their recapitulations.

There is, therefore, no exaggeration in the assertion that key is the main-spring of classical sonata-form. Sense of key is not common to all music, even to all Western European music. It came into Western music gradually, dominated it for (roughly) two and a half centuries, and is dying out gradually—not because it is a 'limitation' but because it is a spent force. In so far as it is a limitation to the free play of a composer's fancy, it is one of those limitations within which (as Goethe put it) the master shows what he can really do. Up to now the atonalists have not found an efficient substitute for it, though Schönberg seems to have thought he might have found one in the tone-rows of twelve-tone music. Atonalists, and composers who have half abandoned key, still sometimes write movements that preserve the general outline of sonata-form as regards sequence of themes—statement, development, recapitulation—but they are like children playing with a clockwork toy after the spring is broken or priests performing symbolic rites whose meaning they have forgotten. For sonata-form sprang from key and becomes mere lifeless, empty pattern when key loses its force.

V

THE CONCERTO PRINCIPLE

I ONCE heard someone throw off a casual definition of a concerto as 'a sort of sonata or symphony for solo instrument and orchestra'. If he had had in mind only the nineteenth century type of piano concerto—the Schumann, the Grieg, the Tchaikovsky B flat minor—he would not have been so very far wrong. Some people would retort that the rightness of his definition as applied to those familiar and over-popular works is an adverse criticism of them as concertos. But that seems to me a narrow and pedantic view. We may regret this twist in the historical development of the concerto, just as—if we are diehard enough—we may regret the invention of valve-mechanism for the brass or all developments in harmony since Mozart's time, but we have to accept it as a historical fact. The point is that it needed a twist in the history of the concerto to make it approximate to a symphony for solo and orchestra; it began as something quite different.

I must repeat—for the last time—that every true kind of musical design springs from a structural principle, from some device for going on spinning music out of a quite small beginning. The difference between the sonata or symphony and the concerto may be stated in a dozen words: the structural principle of the sonata is key-contrast, the structural principle of the concerto is contrast of volume. You can say the same thing in a different way by repeating it in another key; you can also do it by repeating it more softly (or, less usually, more loudly) or with fewer or more instruments, or with thinner or thicker orchestral texture, or on a different manual of organ or harpsichord. The 'echo' effect is one of the oldest devices of instrumental music: either the simple *piano* echo of something that has just been played *forte*, or a slightly ornamented echo. Again: the position of choirs in churches and monasteries, where the singers tended to be seated in two bodies facing each other, naturally suggested to composers the idea of antiphony—one body answering the other either with the same music or with different music. There was still contrast of volumes, though not of different volumes but of equal ones coming from different directions. The same idea is found in such instrumental music as the *Sonata pian e forte* for brass of the sixteenth-century composer Giovanni Gabrieli, organist of St. Mark's at Venice where the structure of the building lent itself particularly to such antiphonal effects. (To play a work of this nature on one body of instruments grouped together on a concert-platform is utterly senseless—as senseless as the playing of Bach's Third Brandenburg Concerto right through by the full body of strings, without distinguishing *soli* and *tutti* passages.) These devices of echo and antiphony are the true origins of the concerto.

Of course, as instrumental music developed they were used in conjunction with its other structural devices of key-contrast and thematic contrast. And, as Tovey brilliantly demonstrates in his great essay on 'The Classical Concerto' in Vol. III of his *Essays in Musical Analysis*, the composers of early eighteenth-century concertos—the earliest true concertos actually so-called—also took a number of hints from the contemporary operatic aria. At this stage 'concerto' was, like 'fugue', not so much a form, a pattern, as a principle. (Indeed one might go a great deal further and say that all musical designs, including sonata, remain *living* designs only so long as they embody certain structural principles; when they become mere formal moulds they are dead.) Wherever you have antiphony between solo voice and orchestra or solo instrument (or group of solo instruments) and orchestra, soloist or soloists echoing or answering the orchestra or *vice versa*, there you have the concerto-principle. The element of display, of technical virtuosity, which we have come to associate with the concerto-style, or rather with the solo-parts of concertos, is not really essential to the concerto-idea at all, though one can very easily see how it crept in when only one player (or singer) was set in contrast with the orchestra.

The concerto-style and concerto-design did not even demand an orchestra for their embodiment in Bach's time. The harpsichord offered a perfectly efficient medium for obtaining contrasts. With its two keyboards, its stops and its couplers, it was comparable with the organ of the period, and the composer could heighten the difference between what we may call the 'solo' keyboard and the *tutti* keyboard by writing a heavier texture for the one, a thinner for the other. The modern performer who plays Bach's Italian Concerto on a piano must do what he can with these differences of texture, and perhaps with dynamics; but as often as not he fails and the concerto-element which is the very *raison d'être* of the music, and which is perfectly obvious on the harpsichord, disappears. Nor should we think of Bach's Italian Concerto as an isolated *tour de force*, a rather perverse attempt to make one keyboard instrument take the place of soloist-and-orchestra. Transcriptions of orchestral concertos were popular at the time and Bach himself transcribed for solo harpsichord at least sixteen concertos by Vivaldi and other contemporaries; the Italian Concerto actually so called is simply an original composition on the same lines as these transcriptions of 'Italian concertos', and the Prelude to Bach's English Suite in G minor is equally in concerto-style. Indeed, if you will look at a copy of that Prelude you will get as clear an example of the typical first movement of a *concerto grosso* of the period as any one can think of. There is nothing very much in the way of thematic contrast. The key-scheme is simple enough: a 32-bar *tutti* in G minor at the beginning, exactly balanced by a similar passage at the end, with excursions into nearly related keys between. But mark on your copy the differences between the vigorous, heavily 'scored' quasi-*tuttis* and the thinner, more delicately written passages that would be played by the solo instrument or *concertino* of soloists in a *concerto grosso*, and the design at once emerges:

32 bars *tutti*.	2 bars *tutti*.
34 bars 'solo'.	18 bars 'solo'.
32 bars *tutti*.	4 bars *tutti*.
22 bars 'solo'.	19 bars 'solo'.
4 bars *tutti*.	34 bars *tutti*.
12 bars 'solo'.	

Of course when put on paper like that, it does not appear very much like a design. But it is not a spatial form; it is not meant to be looked at on paper. When *heard*, it is perfectly clear and satisfactory: a long *tutti* in the tonic key, a long 'solo' in a related key, a parallel long *tutti* in the relative major (B flat major instead of G minor), a succession of 'solo' passages into which the *tutti* keeps breaking with interjections of the main theme (various keys), and finally another long *tutti* in the tonic.

All the same, the complete transcription of *concerti grossi*—or imitation of them—on the harpsichord was, from the point of view of musical evolution, a blind alley. On the other hand another kind of concerto transcription, in which Bach indulged freely, was to lead to very important consequences. This was the arrangement for harpsichord of the solo parts of violin concertos. Of Bach's seven clavier concertos, certainly six and probably all seven are arrangements of his own violin concertos. And so the piano concerto was born. Until then the harpsichord's part in concertos had simply been that of a filling-in instrument, *continuo* as it is called, played from the orchestral bass-part and elaborated with the guidance of figures indicating the harmony. (Even now when Bach arranged a concerto with a harpsichord in the solo role, he expected another harpsichord to play the continuo part with the orchestra;[1] indeed there is a good deal of evidence that this practice persisted till Mozart's time and that Mozart, too, expected another keyboard instrument to play with the orchestra in his piano concertos; the *continuo* died hard, for Haydn played the piano or harpsichord with his last symphonies in London

[1] Not to be confused with his concertos for two *solo* harpsichords.

although no part for it appears in the scores.) But, as anyone who has heard (say) the D minor will remember, Bach's clavier concertos are practically devoid of any element of display; the one notable exception is the solo keyboard part of the Fifth Brandenburg Concerto with its long cadenza-like passage in the first movement.

The serpent of prima-donnaism was introduced into the Eden of the concerto by one of Sebastian Bach's sons, Johann Christian. Whereas Johann Christian's elder brother, Carl Philipp Emanuel, with all his divagations from his father's style and ideals, kept faithfully to the true concerto principle, Johann Christian weakened it in his piano concertos by heightening the importance of the solo part, decking it out with brilliant passage-work, and subordinating the role of the orchestra. And although the greater masters of the concerto, the mature Mozart, Beethoven, Brahms, never lost sight of the real concerto-idea—the contrast and interplay of soloist and orchestra—it was only too often forgotten by the virtuoso-composers—the Hummels and Fields and Chopins and Kalkbrenners, even by Mozart in his younger days—who were mostly concerned to provide themselves with works in which they could display their own artistry against an imposing orchestral background. The next stage—and it begins with Beethoven and continues very markedly even in Brahms, the guardians of the true concerto-principle—is a characteristically romantic one: the casting of the solo instrument in a 'personal' role, quite apart from considerations of display, as a sort of hero leading the orchestra or pitted against it. The modern piano, as its mechanism was improved, became more and more suited to this style—more than any other solo instrument—and so was evolved the characteristic heroic-romantic piano concerto of the nineteenth century: the Schumann, the Liszts, the Grieg, the Tchaikovskys, the Rakhmaninovs, and the rest—some of them written by composers who were not outstanding or even good pianists (Schumann, Grieg, Tchaikovsky). The piano concerto had become a symphony for piano and orchestra.

But, as I have said, even earlier in its history the concerto had begun to take hints from sonata and symphony both in key-treatment and thematic treatment. History—including musical history—is never as neat and clear-cut as the historian has to make it appear in getting his story told straightforwardly. The eighteenth-century instrumental forms did not sort themselves out tidily into separate compartments. The concerto-principle invaded the symphony and produced the *sinfonia concertante*, of which we have some fine examples by Haydn and Mozart, and perhaps helped to beget modern orchestration, and the 'concerto symphony' lived on in the nineteenth century in such typically romantic forms as Berlioz's *Harold in Italy* where the solo viola is literally cast for the role of the hero. Conversely the sonata-principle was adapted by concerto-composers—with most fascinating results. For the piano concerto in its heyday (let us be narrow-minded for once and identify that heyday with the later Mozart) embodies two quite different structural principles: the concerto-principle proper and the sonata-principle; it is consequently the subtlest and most complicated of all the classical instrumental forms, and that is why I have left it to the end of this discussion of musical design. Let us see how this combination of the two principles works out —or can work out—in the first movement which, as in the sonata or symphony, is generally the most important.

I have given above a typical outline of a *concerto grosso* first movement: long *tutti* in tonic key, long solo, mixture of solo and *tutti* in various keys, long *tutti* in tonic key. And I will remind you of the typical outline of a movement in sonata-form:

Exposition $\begin{cases} \text{First subject in tonic key} \\ \text{Second subject in dominant (or other} \\ \quad \text{contrasting) key} \end{cases}$

(all this repeated)

Development in various keys

Recapitulation $\begin{cases} \text{First subject in tonic key} \\ \text{Second subject in tonic key.} \end{cases}$

Now consider the possibilities that arise from their combination:

Ritornello (including first and possibly second subjects) in tonic key

(*Tutti*)

Exposition $\begin{cases} \text{First subject in tonic} \\ \text{Second subject in dominant} \end{cases}$

(*Solo*)

Development in various keys

(*Tutti* and *solo*)

Recapitulation of ritornello and exposition telescoped, in tonic

(*Tutti* and *solo*; final *tutti* interrupted by solo cadenza)

I may add that the solo cadenza, that feature of a concerto to which many of us look forward with apprehension and which we often have to listen to in boredom, was most probably borrowed from the operatic aria. And whether we like it or not, the cadenza is an indispensable feature of the classical concerto. Omit it, or substitute a mere flourish, and you will find that the design sounds defective; the final *tutti* is a volume-contrast to *something*—and that something is the improvised, or supposed-to-be-improvised, solo passage which is the cadenza. After all, there is no inherent reason why we should have to dread the cadenza; both Mozart and Beethoven composed some very fine cadenzas for their own concertos and we ought to insist that, when these still exist, pianists should play them and not some little thing of their own or some horror that is no less a horror because it was concocted by someone with an honoured and respected name. If only pianists (and violinists) would realize that a cadenza with nineteenth-century harmony and figuration inserted in an eighteenth-century concerto is nothing less than an artistic crime, cadenzas would soon be rescued from the disrepute into which they have been allowed to fall. But this is a digression, a verbal cadenza.

Writing on the handling of sonata-form, I have pointed out the heightened value of a ready-conceived framework within which the skilful artist can play the subtlest games with the initiated listener. If sonata-form offers many such opportunities, classical concerto-form offers many more. Even at its most conventional, as a complete 'first exposition' entirely in the tonic key, the opening ritornello whets the listener's attention; for, when all the themes are presented in the tonic key, which is or are to provide the 'second subject'? The listener must wait for the soloist's exposition to find out which goes into the contrasting key. But in point of fact, ritornello and 'first solo' very seldom correspond to two complete expositions, though they always have a good deal of material in common; and the recapitulation consequently is seldom a *mere* recapitulation; it has to combine and sum up, as it were, both orchestral ritornello and solo exposition or elements from them. Or the orchestra may drop unexpectedly into a solo passage, not merely to accompany (for, as I need hardly say, a 'solo' is just as likely to be accompanied as unaccompanied), but to interject in contrast. The very fact that Beethoven's audience expected a long *tutti* ritornello gave them a thrill at the beginnings of the G major and 'Emperor' Concertos which we, who know them so well and accept their openings as normal, cannot hope to recapture even with the help of historical imagination. All these additional possibilities were, of course, thrown away by the nineteenth-century concerto composers who simply wrote 'symphonies for solo instrument and orchestra'; it may seem a pity, but presumably they knew what they were doing and what they wanted to do, and we must judge their work by other standards and from another point of view.

That is the final thought I should like to leave with the patient reader: that a musical design is not to be judged by comparison with some ideal model, still less by reference to any non-musical type of design or means of attaining symmetry, but by the way in which it fulfils its own particular function—which will in most cases be the construction of a certain length of music from given musical materials according to one or another principle or combination of principles inherent in the nature of music itself. For that, I believe, is the truth, very nearly the whole truth, and certainly nothing but the truth about the basic principle of musical design.